Alexander the Great

poems by

Elizabeth Schmermund

Finishing Line Press
Georgetown, Kentucky

Alexander the Great

Copyright © 2024 by Elizabeth Schmermund
ISBN 979-8-88838-487-9 First Edition
All rights reserved under International and Pan-American Copyright Conventions. No part of this book may be reproduced in any manner whatsoever without written permission from the publisher, except in the case of brief quotations embodied in critical articles and reviews.

ACKNOWLEDGMENTS

"For Alexander on Your Birthday" first published in *Kitchen Table Quarterly*, Issue V, Spring 2023.

Publisher: Leah Huete de Maines
Editor: Christen Kincaid
Cover Art: TuendeBede via Pixabay
Author Photo: Elizabeth Schmermund
Cover Design: Elizabeth Maines McCleavy

Order online: www.finishinglinepress.com
also available on amazon.com

Author inquiries and mail orders:
Finishing Line Press
PO Box 1626
Georgetown, Kentucky 40324
USA

Contents

Alexander the Great 1

My Son 4

We Called Him 6

For Alexander, on Your Birthday 8

My Mystics 9

For the Mourners 11

Five 13

I Lie When I Say I Feel You 14

A Ladder, a Letter 16

A Poem for Them 17

A Touch, Not a Caress 18

I Launch Like a Tiger 19

Beach Jalopy 20

"Her absence is like the sky, spread over everything."
— C.S. Lewis, A Grief Observed

This chapbook is dedicated to my son, Alexander, who died shortly after birth and to my firstborn son, Theo, who taught me how to breathe again.

Part I

I know Alexander the Great
conquered after he watched
his father's blood fill
a stadium of spectacle—
a theater upon which
his short life would propel

him outward, eastward.
A strategic move, but
perhaps more untethered
than questing.
Young and willful but also with
no home to return to and
certainly no comfort

awaiting his return from the horizon.
In that long east,
there was no future but
to die young, idolatrized and
preceded to the banks of
that dark river by
Hephaestion, whose body
lay supine and denied burial

while Alexander clung to him.
My Alexander taught me:
It is the giving away
that is the hardest.
It is watching the purple

rising and then settling
in the once fat cheeks.
It is the hardness entering
the body. It is this
battle that no one can win.

Part II

Before you were born into death
Alexander seemed a war-like name
and I worried about what
violence would accompany
your great entrance into the world.

These were during the days
when the future was unconquered—
when it was a reflected thing,
wavering as a straight road ahead
but not invisible.

I could accept
your conquering ways,
evidenced by the sharp heel in my side,
if I would be your companion
and your journey would not forget
she who bore you,
like fat overripe grapes on the vine.

Life was awaiting the harvest,
the next city to fall.
These seconds that were conquered
and bent to my will.

But Alexander would never
return to Macedon, not even
to the northern shore of Egypt,
the lip of the Nile.
You, too, would not return home
but would transform a city,
a home,
into a light on the hill.

It is grief that cannot
be hid even as your
persistence is measured
by a flickering
light in the window.
Many passersby don't
deign to see it,
but I keep it lit
and it warms me.

My Son

In the stone church
where I grew up
there lie crooked tombstones
—cross and bones—
engravings that reek of history.
It's hard to be sad when
Death has passed so long ago.

And in that little church
where I grew up
there is a garden
overrun with ivy,
grasping like green fingers.
A lone rosebush stands
as an altar to no one.

And in that old church
where I grew up,
in the tangled garden
are ashes
—everyone says ashes—
but they are coarse,
enough mass to roll
between fingertips.
As large as infant teeth
and nearly as white.

And in this garden
there are fragments
—they are people—
or were.
I never knew their names
and they had passed
like history and still
the church bells chimed
and the sun rose and fell
and I kept breathing.

And then one spring day
a white bucket appeared
and a small group of mourners.

A hole was dug
prayers were whispered,
fragments were poured.

In the stone church
where I grew up
I pray with the hands
that had clawed at the dirt
—at the fragments—
believing that if my son
—ashes to ashes—
existed with the earth
then I should never
again emerge clean.

We Called Him

We called him into
the hospital room.
I slid from the bed to a chair,
to appear as his mother always did.
A shaft of light burned around us.
A social worker sat nearby.
And slowly we spoke in unison,
without opacity, as they say.
"Your brother died."
He blinked twice.
We choked back animal sobs.
"My baby is gone?" he asked.
He was four.

We imagined four years
between them. And now
the years spread out,
distorted. The math all wrong.
One child would always be
left ageless while the other
would grow beyond our reach.

He didn't speak for a while.
He watched cartoons that
now remind me of
the odor of death.
Then he pointed at my
still swollen stomach.
"Is my baby still there?"
he asked.

And I wondered when
my son would ever again
have a mother who could
answer the simplest questions
clear-eyed, as if
any answers now existed.

Where did his mother go?
I knew she had packed up
and a stealthy substitute remained.
But I didn't want him to know
the magnitude of his loss.

We emerged into a new world
from those neon lights.
One day we passed a graveyard.
He called the stones "gravels."
"My baby is just bones now,"
he said, as the substitute
wept behind the wheel.

For Alexander, on Your Birthday

In spring we tell ourselves lies:
That we understand regrowth
and death, its analogue.
A simple cycle, sweet and round
like a milky breast.

I fear the churning waves as we
pass from one age to another.
You die again each spring
against the seasons.

Each season we bury you
and we come back and back.
We don't feel your movement
and our years don't recycle
or nourish, but fall on bare
ground that will always
resist the buds.

My Mystics

I've visited mystics,
tarot wielders,
crystal bearers.
The future
seethes through
their fat fingers
as I watch them conjure.

A short woman
whose necklaces
drip like tears.
She says twins
—it's always twins—
will follow
with the first sowing
of the unnatural spring
that untwines after
(how can there
be an *after*?)
my son's death.

She was full of it—
of both confidence and shit—
and still that still winter
I manifested:
she must be
supremely knowing

and they would
come—home—as the
plants summoned
buds and I breathed
so close
I could name
them and call them
to me.

I didn't trust
the way her missing
tooth winked
in that mouth I waited
to hear open.
But open it did
and the twins followed:
twins of shame and
desperate mothers
who whisper for
desperate things
that shall never
come to pass.

I began collecting
these women
—always women—
and watched for
the lightning strike,
for the angel's call,
for a hook upon which
to hang these heavy weeds.

There are no trumpets, still,
but one whispered
two boys and two girls
and I've counted on my fingers
those who are alive
and that which is dead
to know I must knit within
myself one more
to fulfill this last prophecy
of a future that is unchanging
and carved deep within me.

For the Mourners

Fuck days of obligation:
The lengthy roads
like bridges to nowhere
that keep spanning and spanning.
Cracked concrete and ripped
stockings that should not
be ripped

and yet they are.
Dog hair and crumbs
and French beans in lemon sauce
that fall on cloth seats
and form a shadow
like a time machine
that you just wish you could
jump into.
Not before the stain

but before these days
of obligation
became obligated.
Before needing to fake it.

Before when everything
could be strived for
and nothing needed
to be left unachieved.
The world was as safe as

a cardboard box in those days.
The walls have ripped
since then and even
around the festive table
I can taste your absence
in the freshly popped
cranberry sauce and the brined turkey.

Your absence brims
like string-up lights
on the prayers that can't
mention you and
that will never be answered.

Five

Your body springs forward,
jumbled.
It laughs where I've suggested
laughter as a remedy.
It twists with a joy not
stolen. Oh, what
a salve it is to
see you delight.

I've neglected you.
I've receded from
your shore. I've tried
to tame the night,
to quell the rising,
always rising.
For eighteen months
I have drowned.

But you are life, my son.
You are powered by it.
Not by vegetables,
but by heat and a desire
to piece yourself
into each minute.

You are still mine
and I love you for being
other than:
Other than me,
other than else,
other than pain.

I Lie When I Say I Feel You

I lie when I say I feel you,
like a deceptive prophetess.
I feed the masses in my house
these crumbs of faith,
goldfish-like flakes of a story
that death has
no dominion.

I did feel you once.
I felt your heel
dig into my deepest side,
hell bent and pressing.
An urgent cry without the
deliverance of breath.
And since then, my son,
you have provided no salve.

I tell my living child:
He is your brother,
you must love him.
You must remember
the unmemorable, the unknowable.
And I pad my insistence with
chocolate cake. I urge the
phone to ring on your death day.
I focus on the lightness of your ashes
and not the crumbled bone itself.

But I let my anger steep like
boiling tea. I urge it to awaken
within myself, fanned by the
space left by you, my new-born,
my new-death, my ever-son,
my ever-loss.
The contradiction feeds me,
and I devour it until no mass remains.

These sad rumblings will tear me apart.
We protect that which emerges
from within us, our dominion.
And yet, you, unknowable thing,
son, you have outreached my grasp.

And I, on your second death day,
pretend you have not flown far.
Who is the motherless child and
whose child has fled? You have not
listened these years: I command
you to come back to me.

A Ladder, a Letter

Your life as a mother awaits you,
as it awaits all mothers.
The first night you realize her body
is no longer within yours, cocooned and safe.
The snip-snip resolving of a tongue tie.
A first night down the hall,
wailing away from your own bed.

I felt those pains once.
It's easy to feel immune these days.
And then the school bus pulls away and
my flesh waves goodbye through
the finger-printed glass.
Or I hear the word "four eyes" and
my haunches prepare to pounce.

I climb up and down a ladder of pain,
each level surprising me when I arrive.
And sometimes, when I reach the top alone,
I disdain those who have safely
remained below.

It's not a choice or a wish.
I remind myself of this each day I summit.
It's much more frightening than this.
It's a letter destined to remind us
that there is no sender.
Not only that—
there's no paper upon which to imprint our grief,
and our hands remain perpetually empty.

A Poem for Them

For many years,
I rejected the stones
that grew in my backyard.
I denied the altar and I wondered
if those who prayed there
needed a rope to grasp or
twine to wind around their eyes.

And then the worst happened:
You were gone.
They silently encircled me as you
were placed in the ground.
They didn't say much
for they understood that words
can be pitiful shadows
stretching long and thin
ahead of a mother's grief.

But they remained.
They had grown their roots in
the cemetery and I finally
knew the appeal of standing
in front of an ash-grown garden
and talking to it.
Whispering to the flowers
fed by my son.

I remained.
I remained
when remaining was
a Sisyphean task.
Not to be nearer the garden
or to stave off the shade
but to dig deeply,
deeply,
deeply
when God's words rumbled
from below.

A Touch, Not a Caress

I've explored my body
in ways I never thought possible
before you.
Yes, you've woven me to sleep
and I you and
each stirring was felt by us both
and together and at once.

But it was after, after, that I knew
what you had done.
After the ripping, after
the purple scar that winds
its way down, unbraided.
I pull at it sometimes. I itch and I tug.
I wonder if pieces of you got caught,
grasped within the fraying
and resealing of flesh

and more flesh. Not yours anymore,
because it can't,
but mine.
Each tugging,
each pulling,
each fear that elicits
from my softer belly.
Each moan I've uttered over
the red flow.
Each touch, not a caress,
but a questioning.
I ask my body:
Will you come back?
And, if so, how will I sustain you?

I Launch Like a Tiger

I tried restraint
and shunned it
after one year.
My bones clanked like
metal then from
whatever beast I could not
let out.

I wanted to inhabit it—
to become the cage.
To entrap, to ensnare
alone propelled me forward

for a time. And I realized
then that the creature
strapping it's weight
inside—
oh, it needed to be let out.

And when anger let sadness
emerge I watched them
untwin myself. Out
emerged a hair-rising
creature nestled deep and
ravished from a long winter
that had kept those
golden bulbs away.

Beach Jalopy

Only the headlights stretch forward
along the winter sodden sand.
One child is asleep in the back.
I stare out at the white caps
and the wind-whipped plovers
bobbing amongst the waves.

And I speak to whom
I must not speak—
for I am afraid he cannot listen.
I tell him of my refugee in this place,
strewn with his absence like
snail-pierced shells.
I tell him how I sought salvation
variously in the waves,
in sweet wine,
in orange pills,
in dreams,
symbols and signs.

I await the sounds of stirring and press
my thumb against the ignition
but no contact is made.
No life thrums in this machine.

And so I grab my living child
still sweet with half-swept sleep
and we begin our journey
across the other side of the dunes
along a black twisting highway
hoping we will make it home.

Elizabeth Schmermund is a poet, essayist, and scholar. Her work has appeared in *The Independent, Kitchen Table Quarterly, Mantis,* and *Gyroscope Review,* among other venues. She is assistant professor in English at SUNY Old Westbury, where she teaches literature, creative writing, and Greek mythology. She lives in a small beach town in New York with her family. More information and additional publications can be found at www.elizabethschmermund.com.

www.ingramcontent.com/pod-product-compliance
Lightning Source LLC
Chambersburg PA
CBHW022108080426
42734CB00009B/1517